W9-CMI-194

4-27-19

JEALOUS

by Kerry Dinmont

The Child's World®
childsworld.com

Published by The Child's World®
1980 Lookout Drive • Mankato, MN 56003-1705
800-599-READ • www.childsworld.com

Photographs ©: Shutterstock Images, cover,
1, 4, 5, 6, 8, 9, 16, 22 (top right), 22 (bottom
left); Mandy Godbehear/Shutterstock Images,
10; Tom Wang/Shutterstock Images, 13;
Wave Break Media/Shutterstock Images,
14; Tatyana Dzemileva/Shutterstock Images,
17; Ronnachai Palas/Shutterstock Images,
18; Iam Anupong/Shutterstock Images, 21;
Patrick Foto/Shutterstock Images, 22 (top
left); iStockphoto, 22 (bottom right)

Design Elements: Shutterstock Images

ISBN Hardcover: 9781503828100
ISBN Paperback: 9781622434701
LCCN: 2018944232

Printed in the United States of America
PAO2395

ABOUT THE AUTHOR

*Kerry Dinmont is a children's book
author who enjoys art and nature.
She lives in Montana with her two
Norwegian elkhounds.*

CONTENTS

THE NEW BIKE

Neil got a new bike. It has shiny paint. He rides over to show his neighbor Amy. Amy rides an old bike. The paint is chipped.

Amy wants a new bike, too. She asks her parents for one. Amy is jealous.

BEING JEALOUS

Many people get jealous. They really want what someone else has.

That thing might be a friend's toy.

It might be a **talent** such as painting.

Jealous people think about what they want a lot. They might get **angry** with someone who has it.

THINK ABOUT IT

What things have made you jealous?

Try to be happy with what you have.

Think about your own toys or talents.

List reasons why you like them.

People will have things you want.
You may be jealous. Do not get
angry with them. Be happy for them.

OTHER PEOPLE'S JEALOUSY

Some people might be jealous of you. They want what you have. They might be mean to you.

Be nice to them. **Share** what you have with them if you can.

People are more important than things.

You might make a good friend when you share.

A **friendship** can last longer than a toy.

WHO IS JEALOUS?

Can you tell who is jealous? Turn to page 24 for the answer.

A

B

C

D

GLOSSARY

angry (ANG-ree) Someone who is angry has strong feeling of annoyance or unfriendliness. People who are jealous might get angry.

friendship (FREND-ship) Friendship is the bond between two people who like each other. Friendship is more important than having everything you want.

share (SHAIR) To share is to let other people use your things. If someone is jealous of something you have, try to share it with them.

talent (TAL-unt) A talent is something people are naturally good at. Some people may get jealous of another person's talent of singing.

TO LEARN MORE

Dinmont, Kerry. **Dan's First Day of School: A Book about Emotions**. Mankato, MN: The Child's World, 2018.

Nilsen, Genevieve. **Angry**. Minneapolis, MN: Jump! Inc., 2018.

Shepherd, Jodie. **How Do You Feel?** New York: Children's Press, 2015.

Visit our Web site for links about being jealous:
childsworld.com/links

Note to Parents, Teachers, and Librarians: We routinely verify our Web links to make sure they are safe and active sites. So encourage your readers to check them out!

INDEX